MOLECULES & ELEMENTS
Science for Kids
Children's Chemistry Books Edition

Speedy Publishing LLC
40 E. Main St. #1156
Newark, DE 19711
www.speedypublishing.com

A molecule is
the smallest
amount of
a chemical
substance that
can exist.

Molecules are made up of atoms that are held together by chemical bonds.

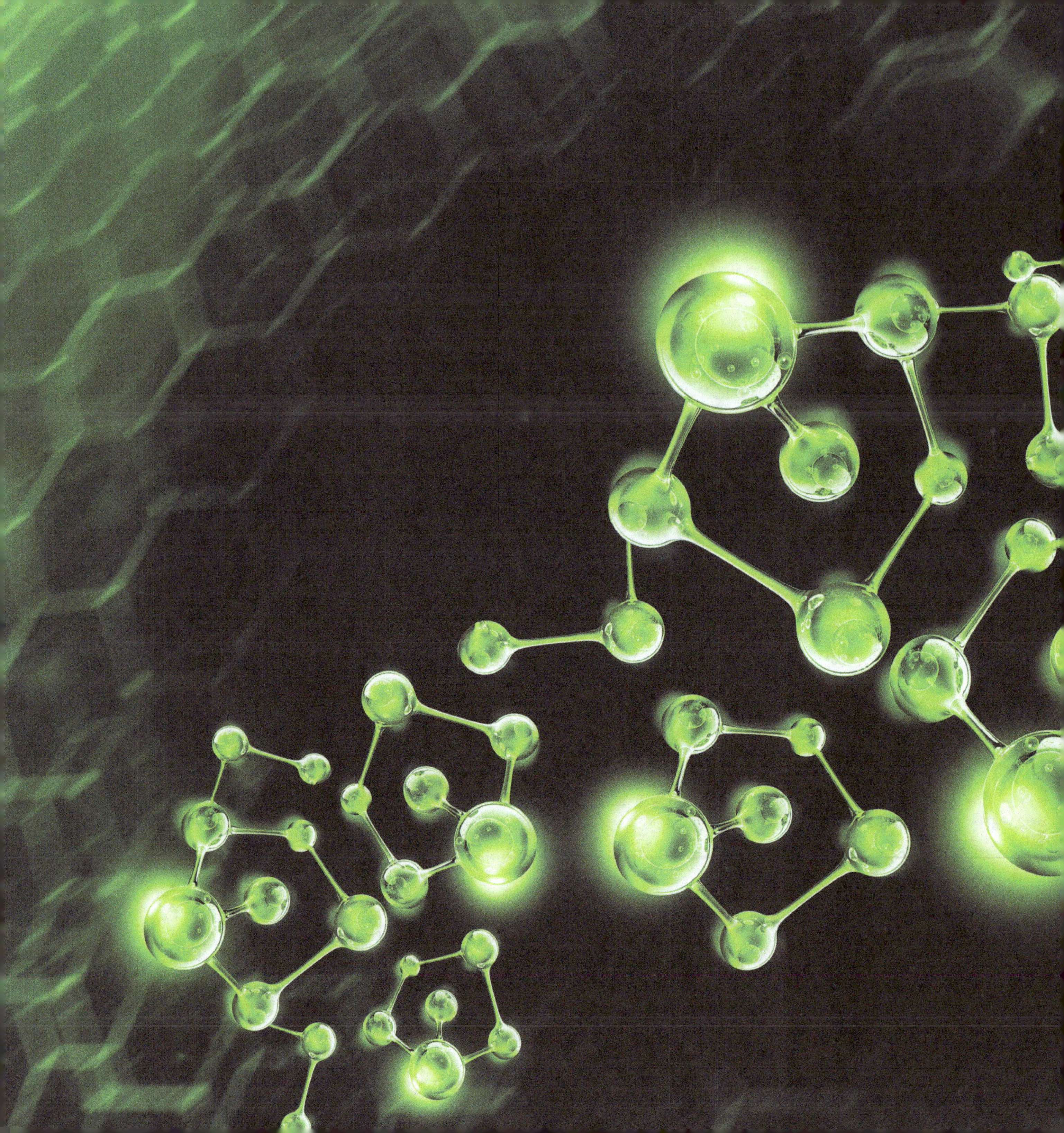

All the stuff around you is made up of molecules.

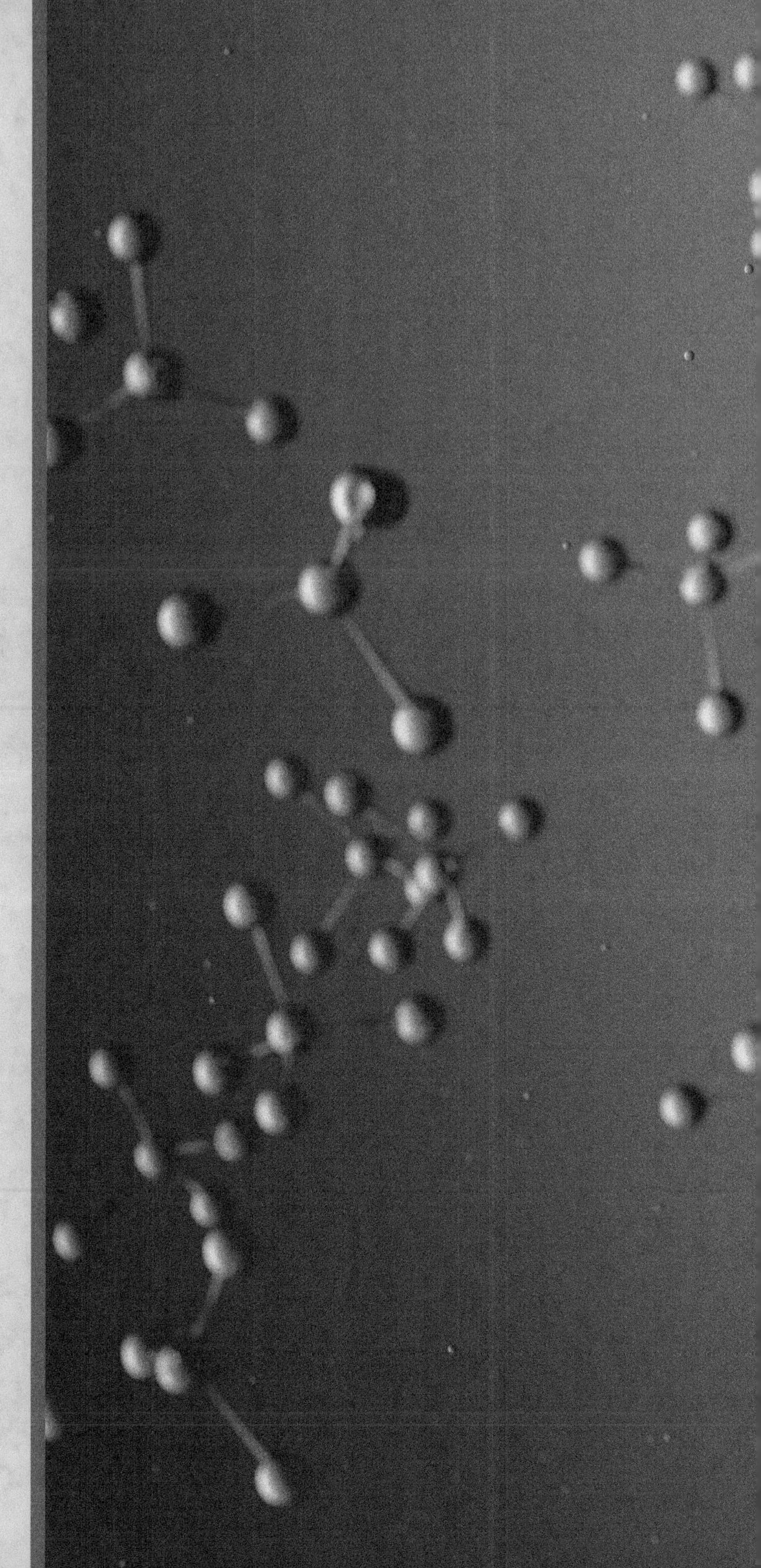
Molecules can
vary greatly
in size and
complexity.

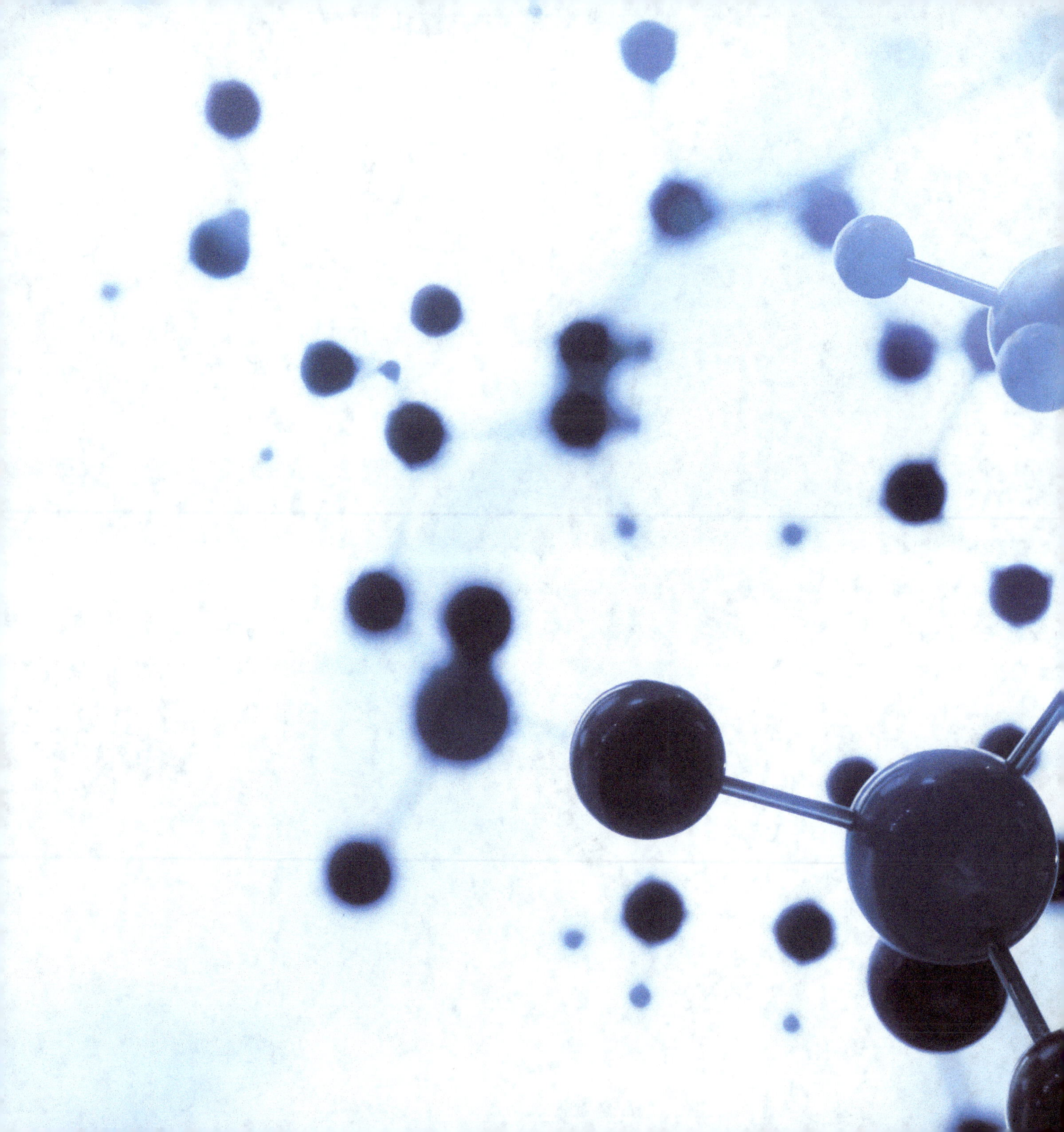

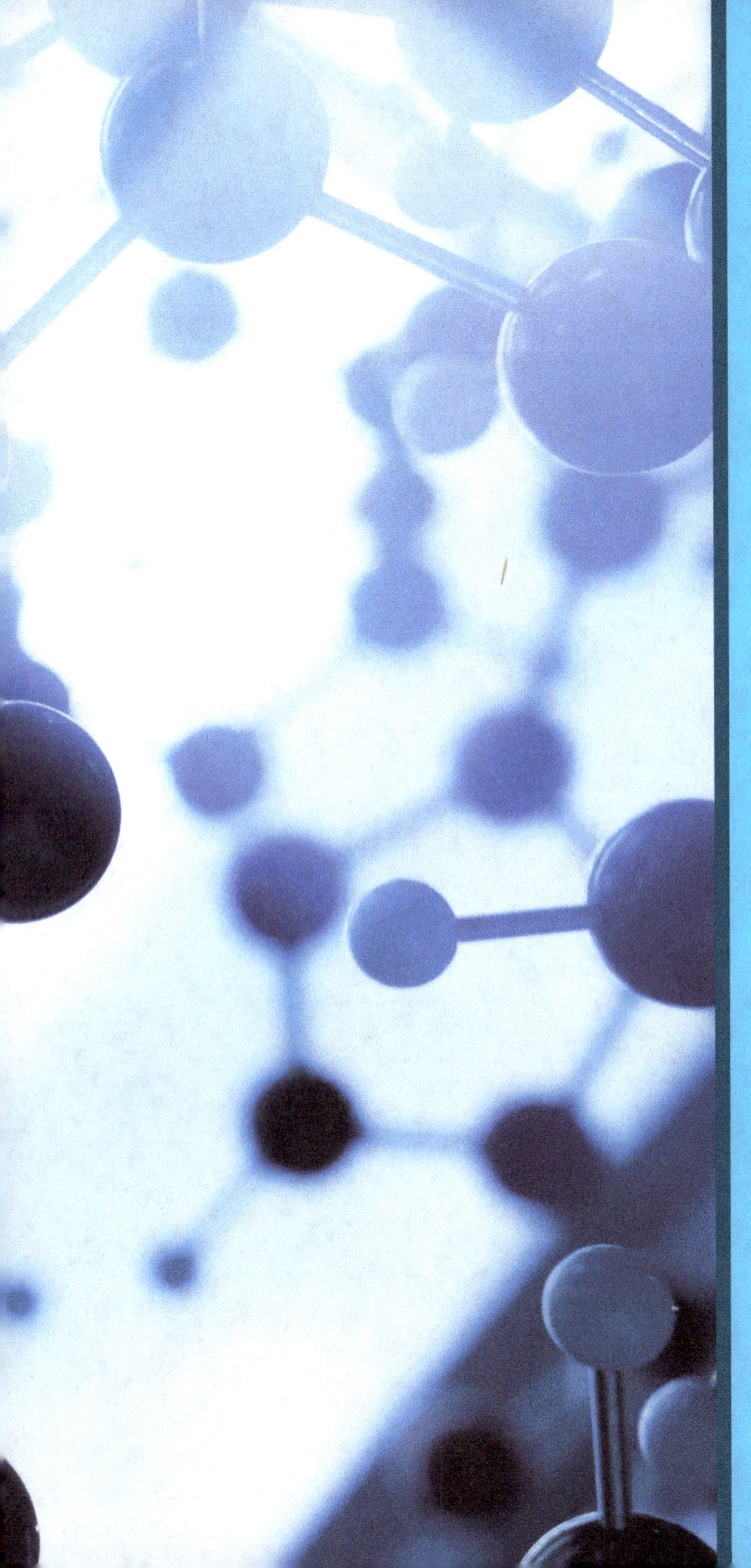

Molecules can have different shapes. Some are long spirals while others may be pyramid shaped.

A human body is made up of trillions and trillions of different types of molecules.

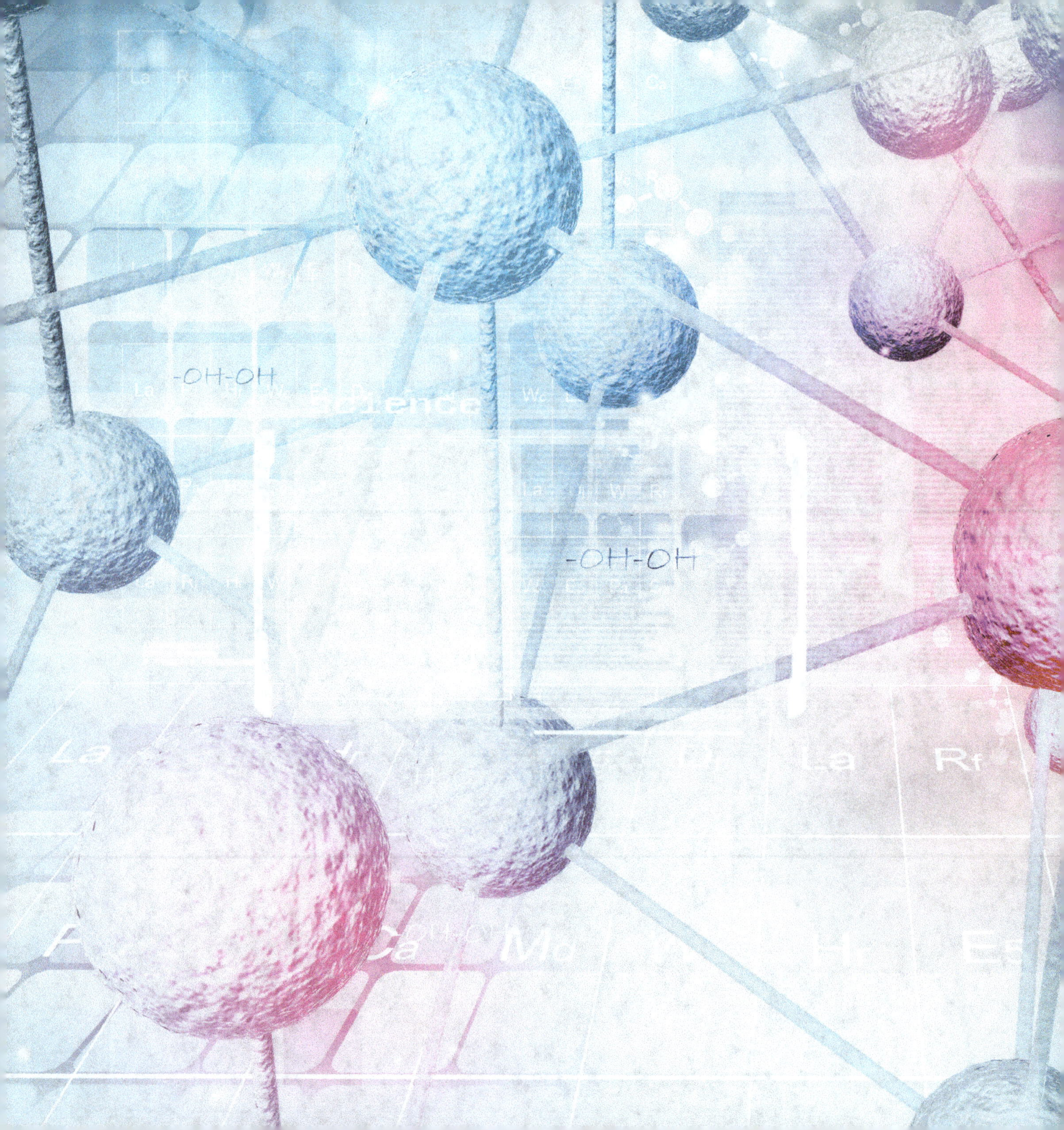

66% of the mass of the human body is made up of oxygen atoms.

Most molecules are far too small to be seen with the naked eye.

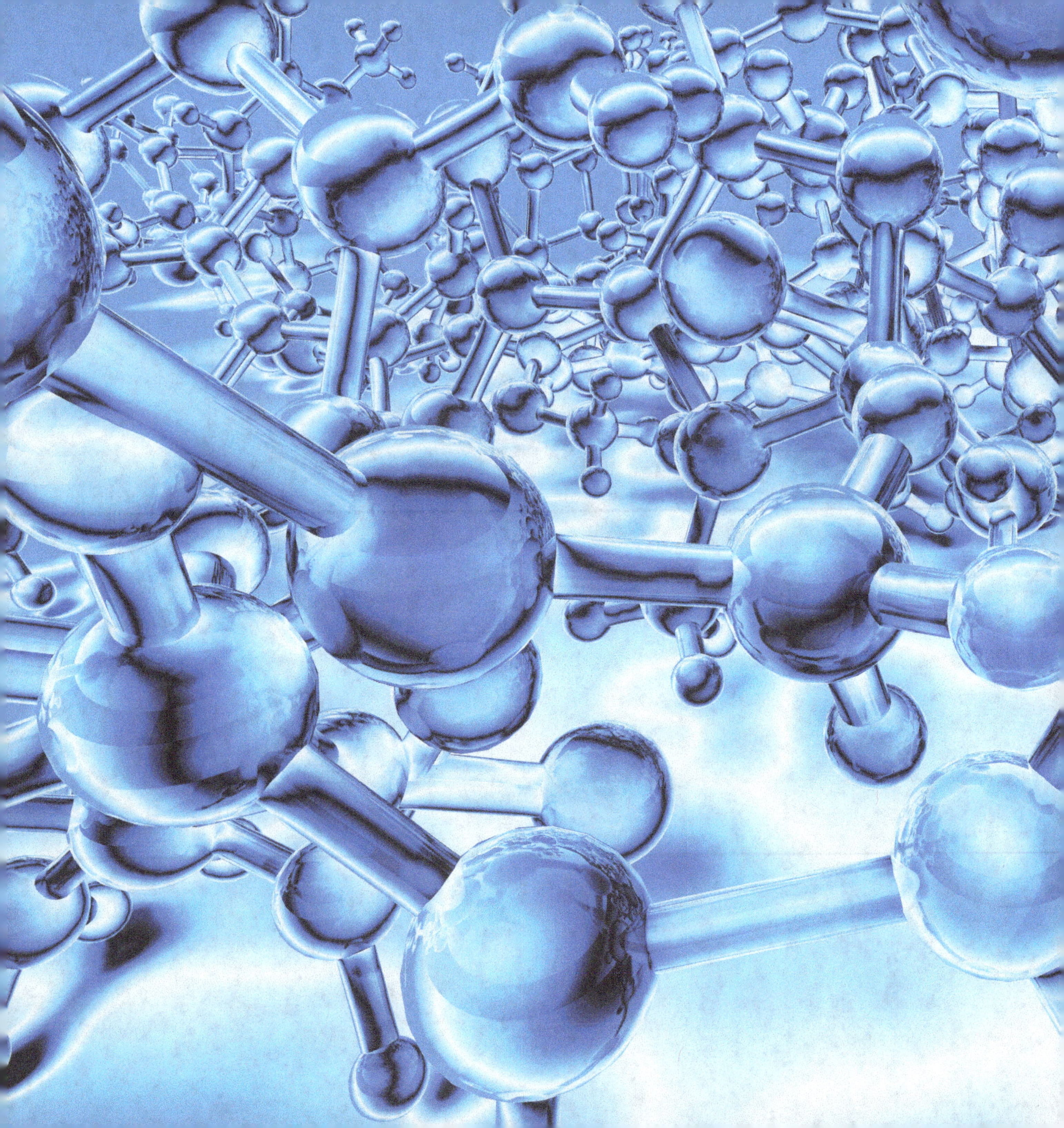

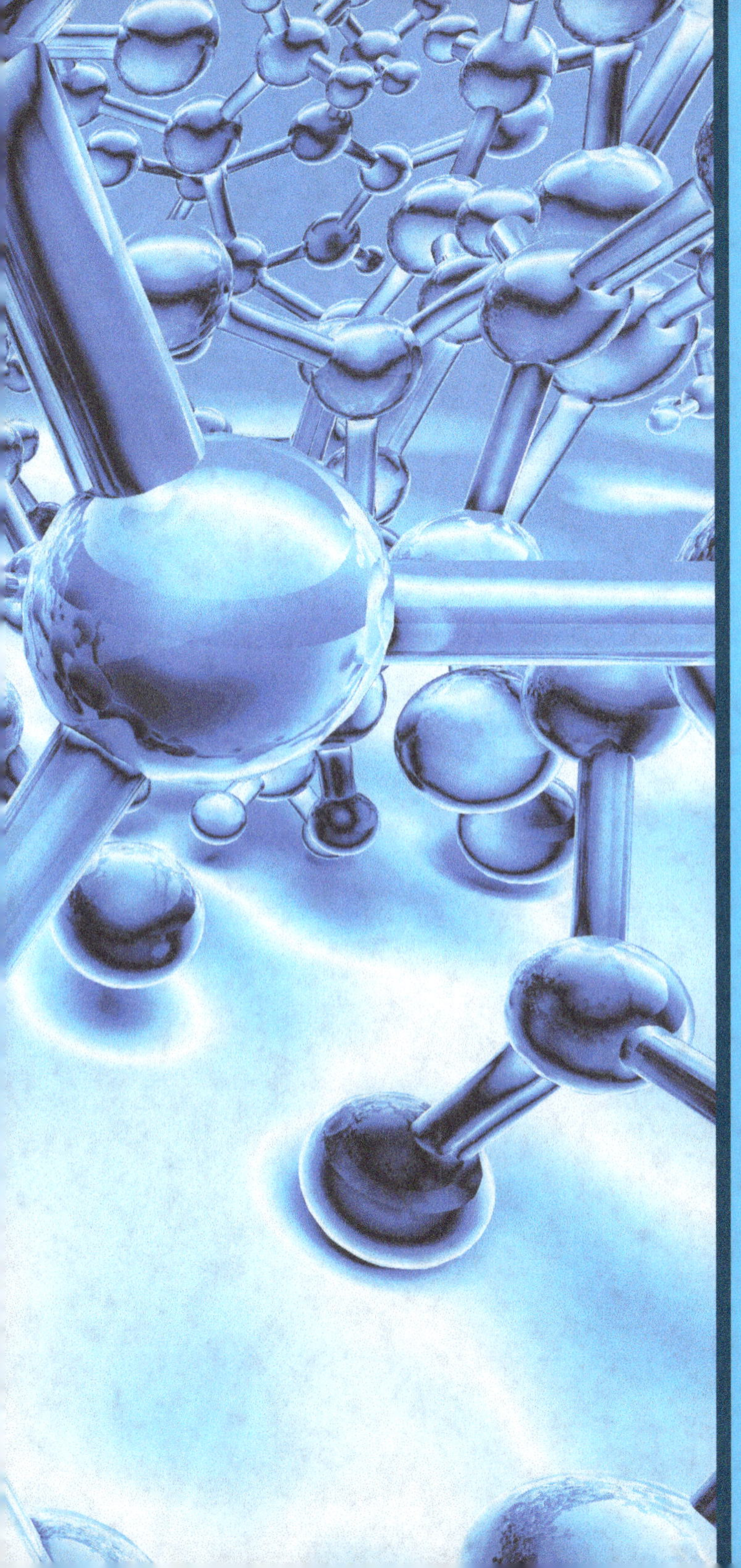

The mass of
a molecule
is called the
molecular mass.
It is worked out
by adding the
mass of all the
atoms in it.

An element is a
pure substance
that is made
from a single
type of atom.

CONH₂
CONb
Sb
121,76
52
Te
127,60
Sn
118,71
83
Bi
208,98
84
Po
82
Pb
207,2
115
Uup
38

Cr
Mn
26
Fe
27
Co
58.933
Nickel
28
Ni
58.693
63.546
42
Mo
43
Tc
44
Ru
101.07(2)
Rhodium
45
Rh
102.91
Palladium
46
Pd
106.42
Silver
47
Ag
107.87
74
75
Re
Osmium
76
Os
190.23(2)
Iridium
77
Ir
192.22
Platinum
78
Pt
195.08
Gold
79
Au
196.97
107
Bh
Hassium
108
Hs
[277.15]
Meitnerium
109
Mt
[276.15]
Darmstadtium
110
Ds
[281.16]
Roentgenium
111
Rg
[280.16]
[285.17]
Samarium
62
Sm
Europium
63
Gadolinium

Elements are the building blocks for all the rest of the matter in the world.

There are currently 118 known elements. Of these, only 94 are thought to naturally exist on Earth.

IB
29
+1
+2
Cu
Copper
.46
IIB
30
+1
+2
Zn
Zinc
65.39
2-8-18-2
+2
Gallium
69.723
2-8-18-3
+1 48
+2
Cd
dmium
.41
-2
49
In
Indium
114.82
2-8-18-18-
+1 81
-2

The atomic number of an element is equal to the number of protons in each atom, and defines the element. Each element has a unique atomic number.

An important way of learning and understanding elements for chemistry is the periodic table.

1
1 IA
1 1A
Atomic Number
H
Hydrogen
2
IIA
2A
Name
Li
Lithium
Be
Beryllium
Na
Sodium
Mg
Magnesium
3
IIIB
3B
4
IVB
4B
5
VB
5B
K
Potassium
Ca
Calcium
Sc
Scandium
Ti
Titanium
V
Rb
Rubidium
Sr
Strontium
Y
Yttrium
Zr
Zirconium
Nb
Niobium
Cs
Cesium
Ba
Barium
57-71
Hf
Hafnium
Ta
Tantalum
Fr
Francium
Ra
Radium
89-103
Rf
Rutherfordium
Db
Dubnium

La
Lanthanum
Ce
Cerium
Pr
Praseodymium
Ac
Actinium
Th
Thorium
Pa
Protactinium

Periodic Table Of Elements

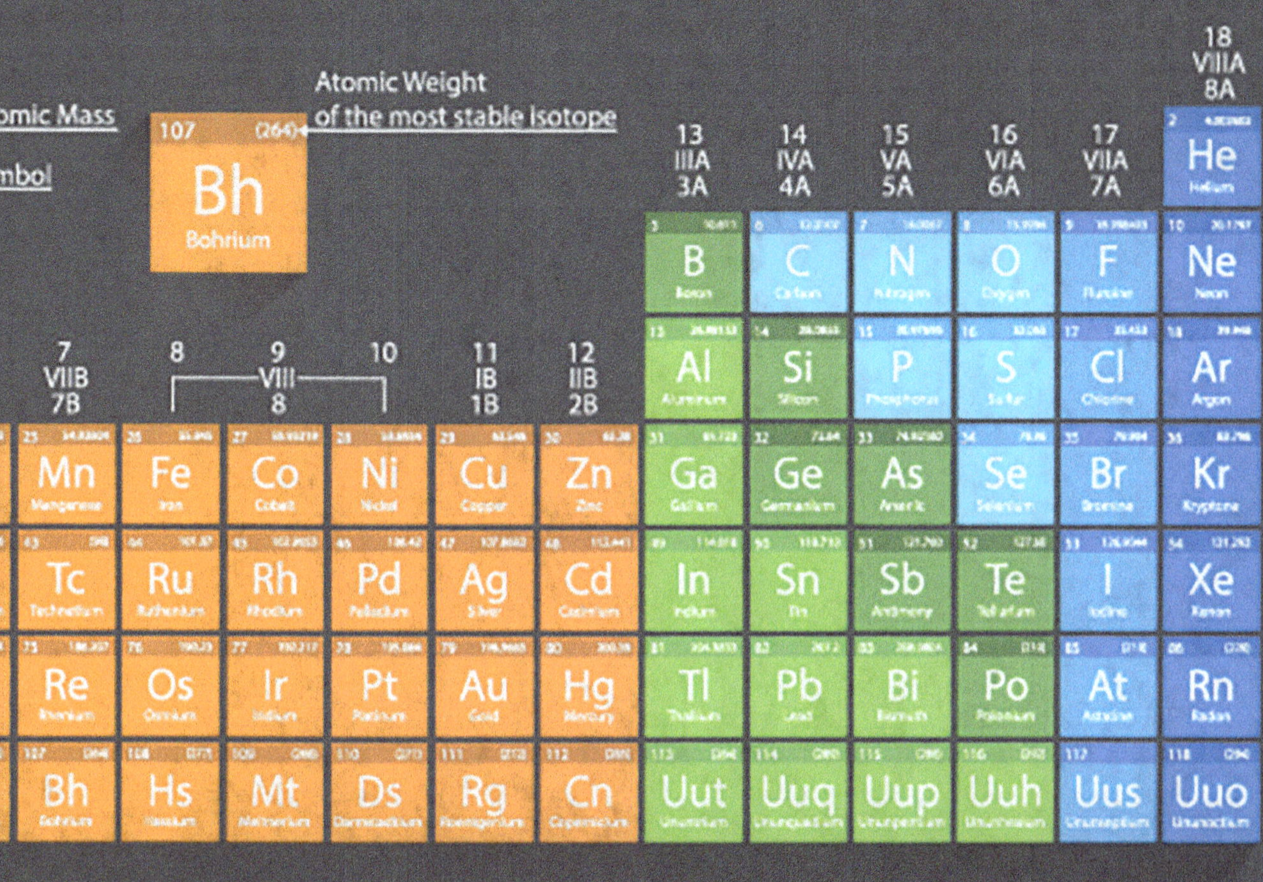

1
H
Hydrogen
1.0079

Hydrogen is the most common element found in the universe.

Elements
found on Earth
and Mars
are exactly
the same.

7 N
Stickstoff
30.973762
31
100
32(8?) 14 d
8.151
2.33
1410
32(β?) 14 d
10.486
15 P
Phosphor
74.92160
5
75
8 O
Sauerstoff
32.0

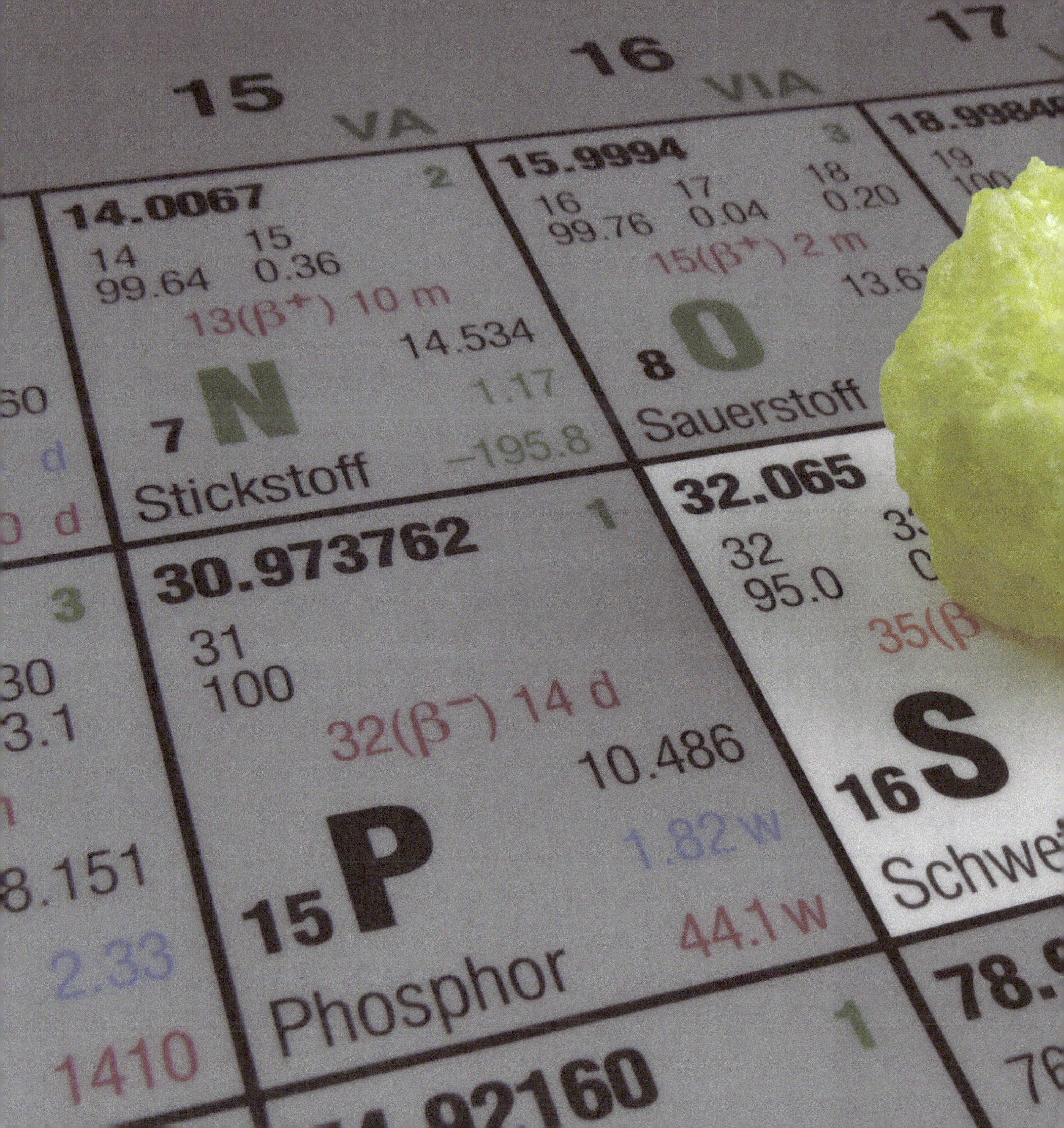

15
VA
16
VIA
17
14.0067
14   15
99.64   0.36
13(β+) 10 m
14.534
1.17
7 N
−195.8
Stickstoff
15.9994
16   17   18
99.76   0.04   0.20
15(β+) 2 m
13.6
8 O
Sauerstoff
18.9984
19
100
30.973762
31
100
32(β−) 14 d
10.486
15 P
1.82 w
44.1 w
Phosphor
32.065
32   3
95.0   0
35(β
16 S
Schwe
78.9
1
1410
1.92160
2
3
60
d
d
30
3.1
8.151
2.33

The known elements have atomic numbers from 1 through 118, conventionally presented as Arabic numerals.

Chemical elements are named after various things. Sometimes it is based on the person who discovered it, or the place it was discovered.

Wasserstoff

2.066

95.0   33   34
        0.8   4.2

35(β-) 88 d

10.360

44.1w

16 **S**

Schwefel

78.96

Fluor

35.45